Copyright (c) 2021
Jodi-ann Brown RDN/LD

All rights reserved
No part of this publication may be reproduced or transmitted in any form or by any means without permission in writing from the writer.

Dedications

To Jaxson,
You are my world, I'm so blessed to be your momma.
Love, Mommy

To Joe,
Thank you for all you do and for showing up daily. You have no idea how grateful I am for you.
I Love you so much

To Medawn & Carlton,
You are the reason I exist. You inspire me to pursue my dreams because you pursued yours. I hope I make you proud.
Love Jodi

This is Jaxson, he really likes ice cream.

Tonight is ice cream night at Jaxson's house with his Mom and Dad.

"Are you excited about Ice cream night?" asks his mom.
"I don't want any ice cream," says Jaxson, sadly.
"No Ice Cream?" asks his dad with a confused look
"Why not?" asks his Mom. "You really like ice cream."

"Dawn from my class says that ice cream is bad for us and that it has too much sugar," explains Jaxson.

"Honey, there are no good or bad foods," replies his Mom.

"There isn't?" asks Jaxson excitedly with a surprised look.

"Yes, instead, there are everyday foods and once in a while foods," explains his mom. "What's an everyday food, Mom?" asks Jaxson.

"Everyday foods have the most nutrients."

"They have vitamins, minerals; they feed your muscles, your bones and your brain."

"They also help you grow big, strong and help you not to get sick," explains his mom.

"Wow!" says Jaxson, "I didn't know that."

"Do you know what a once in a while food is?" asks his mom. "Is it food you only eat sometimes?" answered Jaxson. "That's right!" says mom. "Once in a while foods have some nutrients, but they also have more of the things that we need less of like salt, fat and sugar."

"Is ice cream a once in a while food Mom?" asks Jaxson.

"Yes it is," says his mom.

"I really like ice cream," squeals Jaxson.

"Me too," says his dad.

"What do you think are some other once in a while foods Jaxson?" asks his mom.
"Umm!" thought Jaxson "Cake!" He shouts eagerly
"That's right!" exclaims his mom. "Just like Ice Cream, we have cake once in a while."

"What do you think is an everyday food?" asks his dad.

"What about apples?" asks Jaxson.

"You got it," says his mom.

"I like it when you cut them up and add peanut butter," says Jaxson.

"Peanut butter is also an everyday food," says his Mom.

"I really like peanut butter," says Jaxson.

"So ice cream is not bad for me, It's just a food I should eat once in a while" Jaxson states
"That's right Jaxson" exclaims his mom

"Foods like fruits, vegetables, whole grains, eggs, beans, seeds, nuts and lean protein are all foods we should have in our daily eating plan" explains his mom

"While foods that have a lot of salt, sugar and certain types of fat should be eaten once in a while" adds mom

"Wow, I'm learning a lot about everyday and once in a while foods" says Jaxson

"So do you see Jaxson?, there are no foods that are good or bad." says his mom
"Some foods we eat all the time, while some foods are once in a while foods."

"I understand now mom," Jaxson replies.
"Now, what toppings do you want on your ice cream?" asks his dad with an excited grin.
"I want sprinkles!" says Jaxson "And gummies."
"That sounds yummy," says his mom with a smile on her face.

Jaxson happily eats his Ice cream and is very pleased to learn that ice cream isn't a bad food after all.
He will tell Dawn and all his classmates about every day, and once in a while foods.

About the author

Jodi B is the debut author of Jaxson really likes Ice cream. She is a Registered Dietitian/Nutritionist who is originally from Linstead, St Catherine on the Island of Jamaica. She currently lives in Florida with her husband Joe, and her almost 2 year old son Jaxson.

Social Media
IG: @Islandrdjodib
Youtube: Islandrdjodib
Email: Jodibrd@gmail.com

www.ingramcontent.com/pod-product-compliance
Lightning Source LLC
Chambersburg PA
CBHW042255100526
44589CB00002B/27